poetry & prose from bestselling authors
BRITTAINY CHERRY
& KANDI STEINER

Copyright (C) 2022 Kandi Steiner and Brittainy Cherry
All rights reserved.

No part of this book may be used or reproduced in any form or by any means, electronic or mechanical, including photocopying, recording, or by any information storage and retrieval system without prior written consent of the author except where permitted by law.

Published by Brittainy Cherry

Edited by Elaine York/Allusion Publishing (http://www.allusionpublishing.com)

Cover Art & Poetry Art by Steph Rose (https://www.stephrosetattoos.com/)

Cover Design by Kandi Steiner

Formatting by Tina Stokes

Dear Reader,

A few years ago, we came together to create a poetry collection that showcased the ins and outs of our emotions. We were the girls who felt everything. We bared our souls on the pages, bled out our truths, and shared every jagged edge of who we were with you. We've learned that our struggles, heartaches, and bursts of joy weren't solo adventures—they were universal feelings that many could relate to.

It's no secret that life across the board has been a rollercoaster over the past few years. We've fought against the pressure of societal norms, said goodbye to loved ones, and battled waves of depression. Yet, within this time, we've also discovered new friendships, had seasons of success, and fallen in love.

So many times in life, people only show the highlight reels of their stories. So often, people hide their struggles, making them feel so utterly alone. They put on a happy face for others while wearing a mask to cover up their most sacred, intimate feelings. Yet, we believe that healing can be found within the scars. We believe that beauty can be discovered within pain. For that reason, we invite you into our hearts and minds as we travel behind the closed doors of our souls.

Our sophomore poetry collection has been a work in progress over the past five years. It showcases us falling in and out of love, the storms we've endured in silence,

our sharpest hurts, and our sweetest victories.
It shares our heartbeats.

We invite you to join us on this journey and hope
our poetry can bring you even a fracture of the healing
it provided us. We hope that you, too, will laugh and cry
and burst with emotions. Because, from this point on, we
refuse to keep our struggles behind closed doors.

We invite you into the home of our emotions. Get
comfortable, grab a drink, and stay a while. And by all
means—feel. Cry, laugh, get angry, get quiet, get loud.
Succumb to the deepest and most raw feelings in your
heart. Welcome home, Reader. It's so great to see you.

Now, let's go inside…

Love always,
Kandi & Brittainy

BEHIND CLOSED DOORS

Something in the water is attached to my ankles.
It pulls me down. It makes me drown in every mistake
I've ever made.
The waves remind me of the awkward exchange with a
stranger two weeks ago.
I play the scene repeatedly.
Stupid.

The once clear water is murky with thoughts of self-
doubt that shouldn't belong to me.
The sharks surround me, waiting for me to surrender.
The tides are high. The panic settled into my chest.
I scream, I choke, I pray, I cry.
Attack.

The water is cold, and I want out.
I try to make it to the mainland before the ocean
swallows me.
Something in the water fills me with doubt.
All I want to do is find my way out to feel the sun.

— B

BEHIND CLOSED DOORS

He knew he loved me,
he said.
But he didn't know if I was the one.
He knew he wanted me,
he said.
For now, but maybe not forever.
He knew he didn't want to lose me,
he said.
At least, not yet.
But in the end, it didn't matter what he knew
or what he said
but rather
what I did.
I did not wait,
I did not beg,
I left.

— K

BEHIND CLOSED DOORS

I used to drink you as my favorite shot of whiskey.
Your essence was smooth on the way down.
Your soul warmed me from the inside out.
But it was a temporary buzz.

I gave you up for sober days.
Still, your taste lingers.

— B

BEHIND CLOSED DOORS

When you've found your person, you simply just know. I can't tell you how you will feel, exactly, but you will know. Maybe they'll make you feel the way you did when you were a child, in the safety of your mother's home the night before Christmas. Maybe they'll feel like a song, one you've always known, one that always makes you dance. Maybe you won't be able to place it at all — whatever it is — but you'll just look at them and see it. "This is what forever looks like," you'll say to yourself. "This is where my search ends."

— K

BEHIND CLOSED DOORS

Our framed photographs are removed from the apartment walls, leaving holes that need to be patched. The walls we painted vibrant hues are returned to off-white. Two change-of-address forms sit on the dining room table. Post-it notes mark his and her items. Yours and mine. You get the coffee pot. I'll take the television. I get the vacuum. You take the broom. I cry in the bathroom, covering my mouth so you don't hear me. Still, you hear me. Moving boxes crowd the space where we used to dance at one o'clock in the morning. You sleep in the guest room. I still roll over in bed, expecting your feet to touch mine. Instead, the chilled sheets greet me with reality.

You're leaving first. Your belongings that once belonged to me are packed in the moving van. You place the key on the kitchen island. I stand in the corner, uncertain of how to feel. Relief? Pain? Grief? Grieving the loss of our possibilities.

I love you, I think.
I hate you, I think.
Both feelings are true, and that's confusing.

You look at me, hurt in your eyes. I look at you the same way. We were supposed to make it. We weren't supposed to end up here. Here, in a cold,

dead apartment that was once packed with life.
My lips part to speak, but every syllable has already
been spoken.
We say goodbye with our hearts for the last time.

— B

I liked you better when I thought you were the man you said you were, not the one you hid beneath those lies.

— K

After the last time, I swore to focus on myself.
I swore to fall in love with only me for the rest of my days.
A peaceful life of solitude because past lovers cut too deep.

Then came you.

After years of betrayal and years of grief, you kissed me.

You.
Kissed.
Me.

Dizziness clouded my brain. Confusion filled my soul. How dare you remind me that tingles of desire could still move throughout my system?

Your kiss tasted different than the others.
Like always, with a touch of forever sprinkled in.

It scared me because it tasted so real.

— B

BEHIND CLOSED DOORS

I've realized the more I love, the more I fear. With each new crack my heart endures, I patch it with a silent promise that I won't do that again — whatever that is. The problem with my philosophy is that love is not a house or a car, it is a leap. I cannot ask for an insurance policy, but rather only trust that the other person jumping with me will be there to catch me at the bottom. Or at the very least, hold my hand on the way down, where we will both be broken in unison.

— K

Your hand touches my thigh. I melt into you.
My fingers dig into your back. You press me against the chilled wall of the bedroom.
Our mouths connect. Your tongue slides against mine.
My legs wrap around your waist. You lift me higher.
I explore every piece of your body. You discover every inch of mine.
You thrust. I gasp. You growl. I moan.

We move to a rhythm that only we know.

— B

BEHIND CLOSED DOORS

I loved the way his tongue danced
along my inner thigh,
like a ballerina on stage,
tiptoeing that delicate line.
Spin and twirl, ballerina,
in that tasty skirt of pink.
Remember your performance isn't over
until the crowd is on its feet.

— K

Rage.
Gaslight.
Flowers.
Rage.
Gaslight.
Flowers.

Sprinkles of "I love yous."
Dashes of "I'll kill myself if you leave me."

Then again:

Rage.
Gaslight.
Flowers.

— B

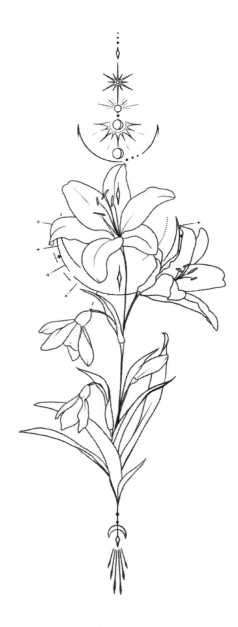

I think this is it.
How scary that moment is,
when it hits you,
when you know that
what could have been forever
is actually just for now,
and very soon,
for not,
and perhaps one day,
forgotten.

— K

BEHIND CLOSED DOORS

A million stars are in the sky.
I want to write your name in cursive against them.
I want the galaxy to swallow us whole and for our wishes to come true as we dance amongst the sparkles of the night.

The burning
flames of
dreams
drifting past us.

I feel a sensation of life when you touch me.
We become the stars.
We shine, we burst, and then we die.

We become stardust as your mess intertwines with mine.

— B

BEHIND CLOSED DOORS

The hardest part about hearing him say that he couldn't see his future with me was that when we broke up, when he said it was the end, he only had to mourn the past year, whereas I had already seen an entire life together, and had to mourn the death of that, too.

—K

BEHIND CLOSED DOORS

Kissing with hate and kissing with love were very much alike.

I only wish I could tell the difference between how you kiss me.

Some days they tasted like hatred; other times, they felt like promises of our wishes coming true.

Oh, how I hate that my kisses love you.

— B

BEHIND CLOSED DOORS

Waking up on the day where you aren't mine anymore is the hardest thing I have ever had to do. If I would have known the last time we kissed was the very last time, I would have kissed you longer. If I would have known the last time I looked over and saw your blue eyes shining and a smile just for me would have been the very last time, I would have taken a photo to keep always. If I would have known the last time you held me in your arms was the very last time, I would have held you tighter, and I don't think I ever would have let you go.

— K

I fight against the morning because the night enchants me.
The shadows trace my soul. The darkness swallows me whole.

Whole.

I once was whole.
Now I am carved puzzle pieces that no longer fit together as one.
How do I fix myself when my pieces no longer belong?
The sunbeams burn the edges of my pieces, igniting intense flames.

Sun.

I fight against the sun because the clouds relax me.
They float over my heart, willing it to pause because it's afraid to start.

Yet, still, daytime comes, and I bathe, I burn, I evaporate in the sun.
I cry for night.

— B

BEHIND CLOSED DOORS

One year ago, I never knew you existed.
Now, one year later, on the very same date,
I wish I could say the same.

—K

BEHIND CLOSED DOORS

I fall in love with you again each time a photograph resurfaces.

I see old pictures of us laughing, of the memories we've made, of the happiness that didn't exist in our final days.

I fall in love with your smile, the one you used to give to me.
I fall in love with the way your eyes sparkled with a sweet ecstasy.
I fall in love with the ghosts of who you and I were.
I fall in love with the pieces that existed before our hearts tore.

I fall in love with you.
At that moment.
In that memory.
At that time.

I click out of said photograph, and I try to return to the present day. I promise my entire being that I'll be okay.

I'm happy that you're gone because in the pictures I never cried. Yet behind those past smiles, I knew my soul would slowly die. The colorful photographs are now black and white in my mind.

Still, sometimes I fall.

— B

BEHIND CLOSED DOORS

What hurts most of all is one day
you will find her —
the woman
you said
I could never be.
And you will stare into her eyes
and tell her about all the women
all the steppingstones
on that rocky path
that lead to her.
And I'll still be here
where you passed me along the way
wishing the road ended here
with me
instead.

— K

BEHIND CLOSED DOORS

You creep into my memories every time it rains
I stop all my actions as your shadows rumble in my
thoughts

You echo in my brain
You paint pictures in my mind
I lose time
I lose my breath
I lose my strength
I choke on the memory of you

You pour into me
Your scents, your laughter, your favorite color
I drown in you

You.
You.
You.

Somewhere out there, you're able to breathe
Yet still, your shadows choose to suffocate me

—B

BEHIND CLOSED DOORS

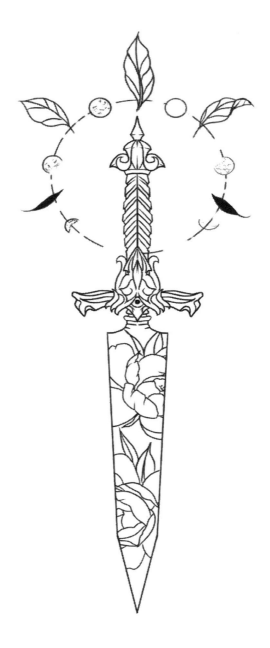

I remember the breakthrough, when I told him I couldn't talk to him anymore. I remember crying, knowing this really was it, that I was truly accepting what he had said: it was over, we were done.

And honestly, as much as he was different, and as much as he showed me this... INCREDIBLE love... that I will never forget... I knew it was what I needed to do. I had to remind myself that it didn't matter what he had said, or done, or promised.

He still left.

He still said I wasn't right for his life.

He still said "close, but no cigar."

So, I wiped my face, and I stood again, and though it hurt as I hobbled in those first few steps, I took them with courage.

And I refused to keep weeping for a man who couldn't see that I am enough.

— K

BEHIND CLOSED DOORS

There's a crack in the attic floor, and I think it belongs
to you.
I'll repair it later, but for now:
I scroll against the brokenness, hoping it won't damage
other corners of my home.

— B

BEHIND CLOSED DOORS

In the movies, he always comes back. He always realizes he was wrong, he was stupid to let her go, he can't live without her. And he comes back.

But this isn't a movie.

And you're staying gone.

And I still love you, anyway.

—K

BEHIND CLOSED DOORS

My heart bleeds when you talk down to me
Yet I still crave your words
Your speech slices into my spirit
Your verbiage fucks my soul

I ache. I hate. I love. I need.

Bruised
Battered
Tarnished knees

Please say you love me
As if those words could fix the cracks that your lips
made

I'll quit tonight
I'll put you away
I'll close off my heart
Lock the memories away

Or maybe I'll quit at sunrise

Just hurt me one more time
One more sentence
One more word

Somehow it always leads to more.

— B

BEHIND CLOSED DOORS

You're allowed to be sad
and cry for what you've lost
so long as you can also be happy
and smile for what you had.

— K

BEHIND CLOSED DOORS

I suffocate:

From the
memory
of you.

— B

BEHIND CLOSED DOORS

I used to believe love was enough,
that it could conquer everything.
He was the first one
to prove I was wrong.
And it only took once for me to learn the lesson.

— K

BEHIND CLOSED DOORS

Why don't we move to Wyoming?
Where night is still, and the morning is crisp.

We'll sit under the stars, trading stories of what will someday be,
and talk about the past mistakes with a gleam of hope for tomorrow.

— B

BEHIND CLOSED DOORS

I will always love you,
he said,
even if only silently
and from afar.

— K

BEHIND CLOSED DOORS

I drown in our memories of who we once were.
There was a time I thought heaven was defined by our love.

Now:

You drink too much.
Drunk.
I cuss too much.
Bitch.

We're in the same room but blind to one another, and it feels so distant.

We have sex and bourbon to embody our sins.
We fight and scream, yet no one ever wins.

When did the butterfly convert back to the caterpillar?
How can we go back to the cocoon and be rebirth?

— B

It was the last goodbye.
It was an hour of laughing,
one more of crying,
and another of being thankful.
For not everyone in this world
will get to experience the love we had.
Even if we didn't get to keep it.

— K

BEHIND CLOSED DOORS

if you leave me, I'll let you go
i won't hold you to a promise you made in a momentary time
when love seemed like enough to carve out forever

—B

BEHIND CLOSED DOORS

Some stories do not get a happily ever after.
Some end on page 38, instead,
the place where you only expect it to get better,
the chapter that seemed to lead to another,
the paragraph that seemed to point to forever,
but it doesn't.
And those stories are the hardest to live,
the hardest to let go of,
and the hardest to forget.
But we love to read them, anyway.

— K

BEHIND CLOSED DOORS

The door opens, and you love me so loudly in public places.
You praise me to your friends as you hold my hand.
Your mother tells me that I'm the one.

The door closes, and you
                make
                          me
                                  shrink.

— B

BEHIND CLOSED DOORS

I'm done waiting.
For you
for them
for myself
to realize that I am worth
more than you say.
Today, I stop waiting
and I start living
the life
that I deem
is mine to live.

—K

BEHIND CLOSED DOORS

I hate the way you made me love you only
to leave my heart bleeding against the carpet
as you shared yourself with another.

—B

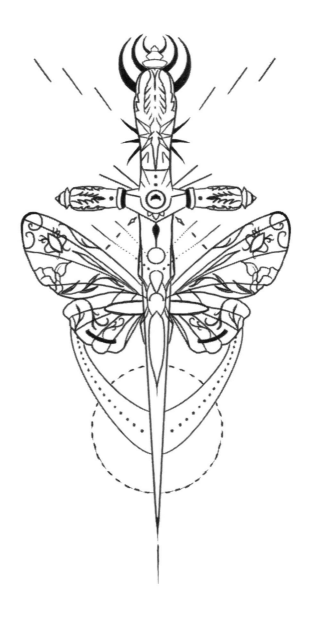

I miss him so bad, it physically hurts. I swear there is this tear in my heart that will always be there and his name is tattooed right above it. And every morning, and every day, and every night, it stings like a fresh cut wound. Like I accidentally picked the scab again and it just will never heal. And I'll be forever destined to just feel that fucking tear like a paper cut on my soul. Sometimes a dull ache... other times so sharp it's almost like being cut all over again.

— K

BEHIND CLOSED DOORS

My door has been cracked by dozens who swung it open without care.
They twisted my doorknob without a single knock.
I was banged against the wall as they tore through my protective screen.
They kicked me shut after hammering against my fatigue frame.

Then, you gently knocked and waited until I invited you in.
Timidly, you opened me slow,
and repainted every peeling piece of me
with a vibrant color
of hope.

— B

BEHIND CLOSED DOORS

Make your plans. Find the woman that fits in that box — that one you envisioned as a boy. That woman who bends and prays, who cooks and cleans, who bears your children in a house on a hill. But life laughs at our plans, and when the day comes, and you realize, throwing your head back as you laugh at yours? I'll already be too far gone to come back.

— K

BEHIND CLOSED DOORS

you can't put back together
the pieces of me that you snipped away
hoping that I would be whole again
and love you the same way

— B

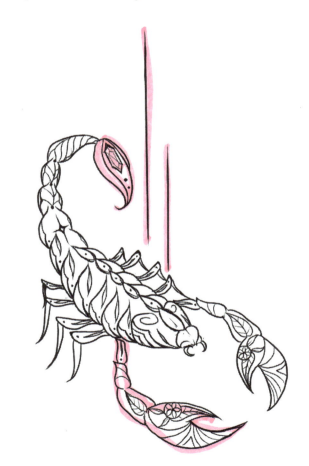

BEHIND CLOSED DOORS

You,
and me.
That was all
I ever needed.

— K

BEHIND CLOSED DOORS

how dare you leave,
yet still haunt my sweetest fantasies.

— B

BEHIND CLOSED DOORS

When I wanted to text you,
call you,
pick up that phone and
somehow reach across the miles,
when I wanted to feel you,
hear you,
see you,
when I wanted to lean into your arms
when I wanted you to fix me
to take the pain…
It was on those days
those nights
when I wanted all those things
but didn't break and ask for them
that I got a little stronger.

— K

BEHIND CLOSED DOORS

When they call me pretty:
I deflect
I avoid
I simply don't believe
I change the subject
I don't take the praise

Because, at one time, the world told me I was ugly
due to the size of my waist and the roundness of my
face

Somewhere in my soul, that's all I believe,
even though so many new people
compliment me.

— B

BEHIND CLOSED DOORS

I wear your hoodie
at night
and pretend its arms
wrapped around me
are yours.

But it doesn't smell
like you
anymore.

— K

BEHIND CLOSED DOORS

His love felt like thunderstorms.
Yours baptized me.

— B

BEHIND CLOSED DOORS

Sometimes I wish I could skip to the next time in my life when I'm completely, blissfully happy and in love. But then I remember that this pain is part of the process, too. It's important. It has to be felt, heartache — just the same as joy.

— K

I fell too fast, without thought.
Like the unstable autumn leaves drifting toward you.
I slipped through your fingertips. You weren't ready to catch me.

You reached out in winter, yet I wasn't ready to trust again.
My heart was frostbitten with ice crystals of the past.

Spring awakened me.
I came back to life after a season of growing pains.

Summer's breeze reminded me of you.
The taste of honeysuckle and watermelon rested against my lips.
We crossed paths again, yet the sunlight didn't burn our skin this time.
We were sun-kissed.

— B

BEHIND CLOSED DOORS

Heartbreak either softens you,
like dough,
kneading you into something so sensitive
you can't be touched without the
person who touched you leaving a handprint.

Or,

it hardens you.
like a mountain molded by the
rushing rivers,
slowly built,
impossible to break,
and only the brave can climb their way through.

— K

BEHIND CLOSED DOORS

Be gentle when you land against me.
For I know how the sweetest taste of nectar
can sometimes involve many bee stings.

—B

BEHIND CLOSED DOORS

Each day, I feel you slip a little more through my fingers. Just like everyone said, I'm slowly letting you go. I'm moving on. Yes, the world is still turning. And I'm supposed to be proud, happy — this is what I should want. But I can't celebrate a world where you don't exist.

— K

BEHIND CLOSED DOORS

if you say you want to keep me,
please promise you'll stay
and help remove the clutter of beliefs that my love
runs people away

— B

BEHIND CLOSED DOORS

The best writing
does not tell you how to feel
but rather reminds you
what you already felt.

—K

BEHIND CLOSED DOORS

I didn't think I'd be able to do it again.

To feel.
To laugh.
To smile.
To love.

The marks he left against me felt like third-degree burns.
He smothered out my joy and stole away my empathy.
He left me empty. Loveless with a hardened heart.

It creeps back toward me, though it was battered and bruised.
Love kisses my ugly scars and calls them beautiful; love hugs my fears until they evaporate.

I feel.
I laugh.
I smile.
I love.

Again, and again, and again.

— B

BEHIND CLOSED DOORS

You came back in my dreams tonight. I thought you were gone from those, too, but you came back. And though they hurt, and I wake with wet cheeks, I'm glad I can at least still be with you somewhere.

— K

We closed out our novel.
I open a new book.
The ink in my pen is still so fresh.
I don't know what's to come, but I know one thing is true:
I refuse to ever write another story about you.

— B

BEHIND CLOSED DOORS

I've written you a hundred letters that you will never read, because I will never send, because nothing will ever change.

— K

BEHIND CLOSED DOORS

He is the promise of warm mornings
after the chills of night.

— B

BEHIND CLOSED DOORS

If I can't even trust you, the only one who took the time to earn it, how can I ever trust anyone else?

— K

BEHIND CLOSED DOORS

Double knot me against your soul when you say your prayers.
Promise me that you'll always keep me there.
Tie me up in your heart, and never cut the strings.

Let me be your favorite pair of sneakers you'll always keep clean.

— B

BEHIND CLOSED DOORS

I can scroll social media for hours
looking for you
but never find what it is
I wish to see.
No posts or comments
or likes or smiles
could ever be the real you.
Those real eyes
and real lips
as they move around the words
I long to hear
"I still love you,
and yes,
I'm thinking of you, too."

There's no app
for that.

— K

BEHIND CLOSED DOORS

My mind floats to forever even though we are only for one night.

I break when you leave even though you warned me of your exit plan.

You never stay, but you tell me you love me as your tongue roams my hips.

How dare you love my taste yet not my heart.

It's my best part, yet you poison it with false dedications.

We do this for so long that I can no longer tell the difference between what's real and what's fake. My soul no longer knows where a situationship ends and true love begins.

So, we remain friends, yet only one of us seems to benefit.

— B

BEHIND CLOSED DOORS

I believe in sun kissed cheeks.
I believe in nights that blend into mornings,
in talking about anything other than the weather,
in loving so hard that the only way out is to break and
rebuild again.
I believe in crying when life is beautiful
and when it's ugly, too.
I believe in making choices,
and not wondering whether they are right or wrong,
but whether which path they might lead me down
next.
I believe in new chapters
and in re-reading old ones when my heart tells me to.
I believe in a love that died when you said goodbye,
and in the love I found after you were gone.
I believe in getting lost in the mountains
and paving new roads
and talking to strangers.
And I believe that having different beliefs is what
makes us all so beautiful,
so uniquely human,
small and grand at once.

— K

BEHIND CLOSED DOORS

The hardest love is
the love that comes after
someone betrayed and mistreated you

But please...
Don't hit the new love
with a bat that belonged to another

— B

BEHIND CLOSED DOORS

Sometimes I read your old texts
or listen to your voicemails
just so I can hear you say you love me
and make believe you still do.

— K

BEHIND CLOSED DOORS

Every happy beginning didn't come with a happy end. Yet that doesn't mean beauty didn't live somewhere within the middle.

Quietly, my mind rereads our in-betweens.

— B

BEHIND CLOSED DOORS

Don't misunderstand me when I say a man can't handle me. I do not mean that a man cannot put up with me, or keep up with me, or exist with me in his life for a long period of time. What I mean to say is I am not something to be handled, to be controlled and tamed and roped in. When I say a man can't handle me, I say it meaning I will not let him.

— K

He's patient with me because he knows that in the past, with others, I've been shown nothing but lies. He's patient with me because he sees me fully when I cannot discover my own worth. He's patient with me because he believes in the road to our future, even when the current path is covered in mud.

He's the rainbow reflecting against my volatile storm. I try to push him away, yet still, he stays.

— B

And I hope I ruined all your favorite songs,
and that your passenger seat still smells
like me.
I hope you can't go to our spot without thinking of
me,
and that you see my eyes in your dreams
the same way I see yours.
I hope you never forget what it was like
Sunday mornings
me and you and a rainy day
spent under the covers
laughing
loving.
I hope you remember,
so I can exist in your world
in some way
forever.

— K

BEHIND CLOSED DOORS

He whispered forever as he nuzzled my neck, the heat of his breath melting against my bare skin as I stayed tangled up with him.

He swore to never leave me alone.
It's his best-kept promise. Even when death knocks on our door, I know he will never abandon me. His love will be my eternity.

— B

BEHIND CLOSED DOORS

Maybe it's because our love didn't have time to burn out, because it was killed when the flame was still blue, burning hot, no ashy end in sight. Maybe that's why I can't shake you, no matter how many months or years pass, no matter how many men kiss my lips and run their fingers through my hair, no matter how far the distance grows between us. Perhaps you're a permanent mark made on my heart from the flame burning out so suddenly, so quickly — just like a star dying leaves a black hole behind.

— K

BEHIND CLOSED DOORS

I think I like you more than you like me.
That builds a wave of uncertainty.

I write texts saying I miss you and never hit send.
I overthink every call and wonder if your tone has a
secret meaning. One that says you'll soon say goodbye.
One that showcases your lack of attraction.

I retreat.
I don't reach out as much.
The gun in your hands is the one I placed there.
I put your fingerprints on the weapon even though I
planted it on you.
The bullets in the gun are aimed at me.
I pull the trigger so you can't hurt me first.
Still, I end up bleeding.

— B

BEHIND CLOSED DOORS

It's in these quiet moments,
when your hands are in my hair,
my fingers tracing highways
between each of your freckles,
our favorite songs softly playing,
you softly singing along,
me softly falling.
It's in these quiet moments
that the universe feels small,
singular,
like it only exists when
you
and I
are together.

— K

BEHIND CLOSED DOORS

There's an album in my phone called love, and it's packed with photographs of him and me. I didn't even know real love existed after hate tangled up with my soul and cosplayed as love—something it could never truly be.

I didn't know love could taste like honey and melt like ice moving slowly down my spine.
I didn't know love could feel like an autumn breeze in the evenings and smell like fresh baked goods on a rainy Sunday.

I didn't know love could look like this: like us laughing in still photographs. Your lips pressed against my cheek. My arms wrapped tightly around your body. Smiles on our faces that hatred could never develop.

There's an album in my phone called love, and it's packed with photographs of him and me. Each time I add a new one, I scroll through my favorite memories.

The stillness of the images brings me home.

— B

BEHIND CLOSED DOORS

I told him I would write a poem about his hands,
his magic, masculine, confident hands.
Those hands sailed around the world,
touching exotic lands,
and chaotic seas.
They climbed mountains in another country,
and made music in my living room,
the guitar willingly submitting —
take me, please.
Those hands have devoured books
fingertips slipping between pages,
thumb slipping between his teeth
to turn the page.

But it was what those hands did to me,
the way they framed my face,
held my neck,
traced my skin,
fingertips skating their way between my thighs,
between my lips,
between the ribs that guard my heart.
"These hands will be the death of me," I whispered.
And then those hands pulled me in
closer
and I surrendered
to my fate.
— K

BEHIND CLOSED DOORS

One day, I won't regret the love I gave to you so freely. But first, the cuts you slashed against my heart must heal.

— B

BEHIND CLOSED DOORS

I have learned that insecurities thrive best when we let them blindfold us and lead us into jealousy, into self-loathing, into uncertainty. Stand up to them. Look them in the eye. Demand answers, scrutinizing and studying and dissecting — and watch them crumble, concrete walls turned to dust, the ashes you will rise from.

— K

BEHIND CLOSED DOORS

He wasn't a prince, and I wasn't a princess.
Still, a fairy tale was built in the quiet whispers of our love.
There was no knight in shining armor.
There was no crown.

Yet we felt royal.
We deserved the happily ever afters, too.

— B

BEHIND CLOSED DOORS

I look at you and I see worlds.

I see the mountains we will climb,
the waters we will swim,
the balconies we'll hold each other on
as we drink in foreign flavors
and each other's warm smiles.

I see flights and trains and boats,
our hands tangled together,
each day a new destination,
each year a new discovery.

I see adventure in your eyes,
and that journey reflected in my own.

I see forever when I look at you,
and the entire world —
our home.

— K

BEHIND CLOSED DOORS

It used to taste divine. A little cream and sugar.
It used to not burn. It sat and cooled down before engaging with my senses.
Now, it was bitter. No sweetness to its taste.
It scorched on the way down.

I miss the way you used to be my favorite drink.
Now you're nothing but blackness to me.

— B

BEHIND CLOSED DOORS

Forehead to forehead,
a touch and a sigh,
a smile and a blush,
three little words brought to life
before never said
breathed into existence by a shaky heart
and suddenly
the world
is an entirely new place.

— K

BEHIND CLOSED DOORS

If I could write an apology to anyone, it would be to younger me:

I'm sorry I didn't see your worth or you trying so hard.

I'm sorry I gave comfort to others before ever holding you.

I'm sorry I belittled you and compared you to other girls.

I'm sorry I didn't tell you that you were good enough.

I love you. I'm sorry. You can heal now, and I'll hold your hand.

I'll never abandon you again.

— B

BEHIND CLOSED DOORS

I've seen watercolor sunsets over white sandy beaches
and waterfalls casting down lush green mountainsides
I've heard music so tender it made my eyes water
and laughter so loud it made my heart swell with joy
I've inhaled the sweetest aromas from around the world
and tasted decadent and luxurious meals
But nothing compares to the sight of you
lashes dusting cheeks
half smile creeping up
Nothing compares to the feel of your hands in my hair
your heartbeat under my ear
Nothing compares to the smell of your T-shirt
the taste of your skin
Nothing feels like loving you
like you loving me
and maybe that's how I know
you're my real adventure.

— K

BEHIND CLOSED DOORS

and i'll play our album on the record player
until the last song turns.

i'll listen to our favorites as the vinyl spins around.

when the needle breaks, i'll let you go.
until then, we'll dance by the fireplace and reside in
the melodies.

— B

BEHIND CLOSED DOORS

They always told me to trust.
Have faith in the path of life,
in the heartbreak and the sorrow,
the gut-wrenching pain,
the insecurities
of feeling not enough.
"Everything happens for a reason," they said,
and I would have listened
if I'd have known all along
the reason
was
you.

— K

BEHIND CLOSED DOORS

I burnt the toast,
you burnt my heart,
and somehow, you think those were equal scorch marks.

— B

BEHIND CLOSED DOORS

I want to know the you
that only you knows,
the one so deep inside
you discover a new part
every single day.
I want to discover with you.
I want to know you at your roots.

— K

BEHIND CLOSED DOORS

I don't need you here, but please do stay.

As the darkened sky hovers and the demons roam around.

As the quiet night whispers ungodly sounds.

Don't let me go until the sun does peak.

Don't call me again until the moon weeps.

—B

BEHIND CLOSED DOORS

When we are at our lowest and hurting, we depend on those who love us to help us out of the darkness — not leave us there.

— K

BEHIND CLOSED DOORS

The hamper used to hold enough for two.
Now, it's limp and only half full.
Yet it no longer holds me down when I carry it to the laundry room.

— B

BEHIND CLOSED DOORS

I'm not saying I can do anything a man can do,
just like I would never say I can do anything another
woman can do.
We all have our strengths and weaknesses,
our talents and specialties,
our interests and intelligences.
I'm only asking that I get
the same respect as
and the same paycheck as
the man who possesses those same qualities
that I CAN do.

— K

BEHIND CLOSED DOORS

There's a whisper of you when the sun rises and sets.
My eyes weep as I watch the colors explode.
The world took you too soon.
As I watch the sets and rises, I always cry.
I know they're your brushstrokes when I see them in the sky.

— B

BEHIND CLOSED DOORS

Life is not waiting for you to live her.
She is not anxious, with bated breath,
wondering when you will reach out for her
and squeeze.
Life
is already here.
She is already happening to you, with you, because of
you.
She feels you as her own heartbeat
and wishes only
for you
to realize the same.
You do not have to go on some grand adventure
taste the most special wine
hike the highest mountain
buy the most expensive boat
or touch the most handsome man
to feel life's love
running through your veins.
You only need to stop in this moment
right now
and realize
Life
is written in these moments
these seemingly silly, unremarkable breaths of time.
This is life.
You're living.
Breathe it in.
And find joy in this alone.
— K

BEHIND CLOSED DOORS

They'll tell you he lived a long life and that should give you comfort.

As if that's enough to still the ache in your soul. As if it eases the fact that your loved one will no longer be there to:

Answer when you call.

Make you laugh when you're feeling down.

Hug you when you need them the most.

It's always too soon when it comes to death.

Old age doesn't make it easier.

It just means there are more memories to mourn and more sadness that lingers.

— B

BEHIND CLOSED DOORS

It's the simple things in life
that I hold most valuable:
whiskey and a notebook and an old ink pen,
a long hike in the woods,
the way your face looks
as light plays with shadow from
the fire you built for us.
These things are what are worth millions.
These simple pleasures are what make me rich.

— K

BEHIND CLOSED DOORS

No one talks about the pause. The period from when someone passes away to the actual funeral. When your emotions are a wave of ups and downs. When you're snappy at stupid things, and can't focus, and can't sleep or eat. You're sad but also numb. You try to go on like everything's normal when truly nothing is the same.

Then it's the night before:

Reality sets in, and you're left with a heavy heart that's exhausted from a week of unsteady turmoil. That heavy heart is trying to remember how to beat correctly again, and you kind of figure that the beats will always be a little uneven because they are missing a very important person who used to control them.

The interlude of loss feels empty.
Yet somehow, it's heavy, too.

— B

BEHIND CLOSED DOORS

Why do they call it heartache?
As if that pain is just a sort of buzz under the skin,
as if it can be forgotten about, with a little effort,
as if it can be masked by a pill
or a drink
or a softly spoken "there there."
As if that pain doesn't shred you into meaty, blood-soaked ribbons.
As if it doesn't steal every new breath, leaving you in a constant state of suffocation.
As if anything can help it, or dull it,
other than Time,
our slowest, least empathetic friend.

— K

BEHIND CLOSED DOORS

I'll melt into you as you caress the loudest parts of my anxiety.

When I say I'm too much, you'll hold me tighter.

When I say you're better without me, you'll pull me in closer.

When I say I love you, you'll say, "I love you more."

And I'll say, "I love you more than your more."

And that's what love is to me.

More, more, more…

— B

BEHIND CLOSED DOORS

My favorite romance is the one
where the girls and the boys
grow into women and men
who hurt each other incessantly until they all have
similar battle wounds.
And then
only then
do they open their arms to each other
and say "you have earned me now,
and I have earned you."
And they embrace,
falling into love
for as much time as they
can steal
before the earth realizes
and wraps them in her embrace, too,
pulling them down,
scars and all,
until they're one with the soil that grew them.

— K

BEHIND CLOSED DOORS

There are crumbs at the bottom of the cookie jar,
and you feed them to me as if they are whole pieces.
Little bits of chocolate chips, little bites of oatmeal.

Little pieces of your love that you try to convince me
is enough.
Still, I starve.

— B

I do not love you anymore
but I still think of you
when the moon and the clouds
dance the same way they did
that night you kissed me
for the first time
outside that bar.
I don't love you anymore,
but I still think of you,
and smile.

— K

BEHIND CLOSED DOORS

You asked me to follow you down the unpaved road.
You told me it would be adventurous.

"Trust me," you whispered. "Let me lead," you begged.
I followed.
I waited.
I stood by your side.
I bent to you and allowed you the space to lead.

Then, you drove us to the ditch.
We crashed.
We fought.
We screamed.
We cried.

Somehow, you blamed me for not being the independent
woman you needed me to be.

— B

BEHIND CLOSED DOORS

I've found that loving myself
isn't as easy as commanding it so.
I cannot just say it aloud,
or tell a friend,
or boast it in a social media caption.
Much like a marriage,
I am in a constant commitment to
that sad eyed
critical
girl in the mirror.
I must love her not just on her best days
but on her worst.
I must tell her she is not a failure.
She is not behind.
She is not fat or old or
washed up
or played out.
Loving that girl is the hardest thing I do each morning,
but my favorite item ticked off the list
each night.

— K

BEHIND CLOSED DOORS

The deranged wolf howls at the moon as if it's crying to be heard.

The broken me screams at you as if I'm begging to be seen.

The wild beast within me pleads for your attention.

— B

BEHIND CLOSED DOORS

Your journey is yours and yours alone.
Do not compare yourself to the
lion, who rules a kingdom,
or the fire, who burns a shining light,
or the hawk, who flies free,
or the wise oak, standing tall in her fortress.
Walk in your own shoes
and inhale the beauty
that you are the only one who will ever live
these beautiful highs
and these gut wrenching lows.
Your journey is yours and yours alone.

— K

BEHIND CLOSED DOORS

And I hope they remember me as a blessing to their life that was solely passing through. Something that wasn't meant for forever, yet still mattered.

— B

BEHIND CLOSED DOORS

I am both
ecstatically married to my life of
routine and health and stability
as I am passionately devoted
to the idea of
abandoning it all
in the name
of adventure.

— K

BEHIND CLOSED DOORS

I slowly unpeel you from the corners of my life where you once so comfortably lived.
Clicking to unfollow on every social platform.
Blocking your number.
Deleting your face from my camera roll.

Each peel slices into my heart as the broken pieces shatter a little more.
I stop crying to my friends over you.
I still cry in the shower, but that's only on Sundays when the day is slow and the emotions are loud. Mondays are better. I keep myself busy.

Unpeeling takes work, so I give myself time.
I'll heal once every piece of you is unattached to me.

— B

BEHIND CLOSED DOORS

Who are you when no one is around?

What makes you smile in your heart,
makes you feel light in your soul,
makes you feel at home in your mind?

When the world isn't there screaming at you
from phone screens
and TV screens
and magazines,
when you can't hear them
tell you what should make you happy,
what you should look like,
how you should behave…

Who are you then?

Are you as free as you were when you were but a child?
Do you laugh and delight in what the world has given
you? Do you love your body,
what it continues to do for you,
how it provides for you to take
this breath…
and this one, too?

Do you admit your love without fear,
and embrace your fears without worry?

BEHIND CLOSED DOORS

Do you get real
and honest
with yourself,
apologizing to those you've hurt
and forgiving those who have hurt you?

Do you close your eyes
and soak in the sun's glow,
listen to the river
as it reminds you
that you are enough
just as you are,
talk to the wind
as it whispers
that everything will be okay?

When you shut out all the noise,
when you come back to the
universe within…

Who are you?

— K

BRITTAINY CHERRY AND KANDI STEINER

Thank you for reading our little book of poetry. If you enjoyed it, please take a moment to write a review – we'd love to see your thoughts. And if you post anything on social media, make sure to tag us so we can share!

We'd love to take this chance to introduce you to our novels.

More from Brittainy Cherry

The Compass Series
Southern Storms (book 1)
Eastern Lights (book 2)
Western Waves (book 3)
Northern Stars (book 4)

This series is one packed with love. Although they can all be read as standalones, the best way to enjoy them is to read in order, starting with Southern Storms then Eastern Lights, followed by Western Waves, ending with Northern Stars! This series of characters will have you experiencing all the emotions.

The Mixtape
A powerful and emotionally gripping friends to lovers featuring a broken rock stare and a single mom healing through his music.

The Wreckage of Us
An opposites attract romance brimming with emotion, second chances, and finding a safe place to land.

More from Kandi Steiner

A Love Letter to Whiskey
(AN AMAZON TOP 10 BESTSELLER)
An angsty, emotional romance between two lovers fighting the curse of bad timing.
Read *Love, Whiskey* **– Jamie's side of the story and an extended epilogue – in the new Fifth Anniversary Edition!**

The Becker Brothers Series
On the Rocks (book 1)
Neat (book 2)
Manhattan (book 3)
Old Fashioned (book 4)
Four brothers finding love in a small Tennessee town that revolves around a whiskey distillery with a dark past — including the mysterious death of their father.

Make Me Hate You
Jasmine has been avoiding her best friend's brother for years, but when they're both in the same house for a wedding, she can't resist him — no matter how she tries.

And if you liked this book of poems, you'll love our first collection: *A Love Letter from the Girls Who Feel Everything.*

Meet the Authors

Brittainy Cherry is an international and Amazon #1 bestselling author of 20+ novels. Brittainy grew up with seven siblings in Milwaukee, Wisconsin, surrounded by love and creativity. She was a very shy, quiet girl when she was outside of my house, but when it came to being at home, she was talking nonstop. Being a shy school student made her excellent at people watching, though, which led to writing her first romance novel when she was fourteen years old. She was too shy to actually speak to her crush at the time, so instead, she wrote a romance story filled with make believe. From that point on, she fell in love with writing romance novels.

Brittainy went to Carroll University for a degree in Theater Arts (in an attempt to break out of her shy shell) paired with a Creative Writing minor. Thankfully, she was able to put that degree to use! Brittainy still cannot believe that she writes love stories for a living. Fourteen-year-old Brittainy would be so proud! Brittainy still resides in Wisconsin with her pets, and her family is not too far away. After all these years, she is even more in love with romance novels, and has a million more ideas that she cannot wait to share with you all. Hopefully you'll find the happily ever after you're in search of.

CONNECT WITH BRITTAINY:

FACEBOOK: facebook.com/BrittainyCherryAuthor
FACEBOOK READER GROUP: facebook.com/groups/brittainycherrygoldens
INSTAGRAM: instagram.com/bcherryauthor/
TIKTOK: tiktok.com/@brittainycherryauthor
WEBSITE: https://bcherrybooks.com/

Kandi Steiner is an Amazon Top 5 bestselling author and whiskey connoisseur living in Tampa, FL. Best known for writing "emotional rollercoaster" stories, she loves bringing flawed characters to life and writing about real, raw romance — in all its forms. No two Kandi Steiner books are the same, and if you're a lover of angsty, emotional, and inspirational reads, she's your gal.

An alumna of the University of Central Florida, Kandi graduated with a double major in Creative Writing and Advertising/PR with a minor in Women's Studies. She started writing back in the 4th grade after reading the first Harry Potter installment. In 6th grade, she wrote and edited her own newspaper and distributed to her classmates. Eventually, the principal caught on and the newspaper was quickly halted, though Kandi tried fighting for her "freedom of press."

She took particular interest in writing romance after college, as she has always been a diehard hopeless romantic, and likes to highlight all the challenges of love as well as the triumphs.

When Kandi isn't writing, you can find her reading books of all kinds, planning her next adventure, or pole dancing (yes, you read that right). She enjoys live music, traveling, playing with her fur babies and soaking up the sweetness of life.

CONNECT WITH KANDI:

NEWSLETTER: kandisteiner.com/newsletter

FACEBOOK: facebook.com/kandisteiner

FACEBOOK READER GROUP (Kandiland): facebook.com/groups/kandilandks

INSTAGRAM: Instagram.com/kandisteiner

TIKTOK: tiktok.com/@authorkandisteiner

TWITTER: twitter.com/kandisteiner

PINTEREST: pinterest.com/authorkandisteiner

WEBSITE: www.kandisteiner.com

Kandi Steiner may be coming to a city near you! Check out her "events" tab to see all the signings she's attending in the near future: www.kandisteiner.com/events

Meet the Artist.

We'd also like to take this moment to recognize the brilliant artist who provided the gorgeous art on our cover and inside these pages with our poetry. Please check out Steph Rose online and, if you're ever in the Tampa area, consider her for your next tattoo.

www.stephrosetattoos.com/

Printed in Great Britain
by Amazon